Cornerstones of Freedom

The Changing White House

BARBARA SILBERDICK FEINBERG

CHILDREN'S PRESS®
A Division of Grolier Publishing
New York • London • Hong Kong • Sydney
Danbury, Connecticut

#1170

Visit Children's Press on the Internet at:
http://publishing.grolier.com

Library of Congress Cataloging-in-Publication Data

Feinberg, Barbara Silberdick.
    The Changing White House / Barbara Silberdick Feinberg.
       p. cm.—(Cornerstones of freedom)
    Includes index.
    Summary: Describes the White House through the years and the
changes made by its different inhabitants.
    ISBN 0-516-21651-1 (lib.bdg.)   0-516-27164-4 (pbk.)
       1. White House (Washington, D.C.)—History—Juvenile literature.
2. Washington (D.C.)—Buildings, structures, etc.—Juvenile literature.
[1. White House (Washington, D.C.) 2. Presidents.]
I. Title. II. Series.
F204.W5 F45 2000
975.3—dc21
                                                      99-052353

On November 1, 2000, the White House celebrated its two hundredth birthday. This landmark building receives about 6,000 visitors a day from all over the world. For them, it is a museum of American history and an important part of the United States government. Its furnishings and decorations reflect the nation's past. Within its walls, presidents have made many historic decisions and continue to lead the nation. Presidents also entertain foreign leaders, government officials, and talented Americans in the White House. Above all, it is the home of the president of the United States and the First Family.

Today's White House is not the original structure, built in the late 1700s. Over the past two centuries, the president's house has been reconstructed and remodeled to make it more attractive, spacious, and modern. Presidential couples have installed the latest inventions and technology of their times for the sake of comfort and efficiency. Not only has the mansion changed tremendously, so have the people who work there. Through it all, though, the White House still resembles the historic structure planned by George Washington.

George and Martha Washington were the only presidential couple who did not live in the White House. From 1789 to 1790, the Washingtons rented houses in New York City, the temporary capital of the United States. Then, when the U.S. government moved to

The plan for Washington, D.C., shows that in the late 1700s, the White House was close to the Potomac River. After the mansion was built, a section of the river was filled, creating more land in the city.

Philadelphia, they lived in a friend's mansion. Meanwhile, plans were made to relocate the government to a new capital city on the banks of the Potomac River, soon to be called Washington, D.C.

In these plans, George Washington wanted to make sure that future First Families had a suitable home in the new capital. In March 1792, he took Secretary of State Thomas Jefferson's advice and held a contest to find the best design for the president's new house. The president and a board of federal commissioners thoroughly examined nine competing plans. After looking at the first two entries, the president commented that "if none more elegant than these should appear . . . the exhibition of architecture will be a dull one indeed."

The commissioners rejected drawings of tall, square buildings modeled on plantation houses, courthouses, or town halls. On July 17, 1792, they awarded the prize—the winner's choice of either $500 or a gold medal—to James Hoban, an Irish-born architect from Charleston, South Carolina. He took the gold medal.

James Hoban's design for the exterior of the White House

As the president's house was being built, Hoban worked closely with Washington and accepted his suggestions. Washington preferred two stories instead of the three in Hoban's original design. Washington also wanted stone walls. For the interior, Hoban designed a room—the East Room—similar to the banquet room at Mount Vernon, Washington's plantation. The East Room was intended to hold large numbers of guests and was located across one end of the building. The Executive

The East Room. James Hoban called it the "Public Audience Room."

Mansion was widened and deepened, and stone ornaments were added to the outside. In 1798, the outer walls were whitewashed. Is it any wonder that the public began to call it the "White House"? In its final form, the president's house was 168 feet (51.2 meters) across and 85 feet (25.9 m) deep.

As the first presidential couple to live in the White House, President John Adams and his

wife, Abigail, ordered the first of many improvements to the building. On November 1, 1800, they moved in and soon discovered that only six of the thirty rooms had plaster on the walls—and some of the plaster was still wet. In addition, the main and back staircases were not installed, and the house was damp and drafty.

In a letter to her sister, Abigail complained, "We have not the least fence, yard, or other conveniences without, and the great unfinished audience room [the East Room] I make a drying-room of, to hang clothes in." The Executive Mansion offered so little protection from the wind and rain that the ceiling of the East Room soon collapsed. Congress agreed to fix up the president's house. A workman even built an outdoor toilet for the Adamses. Until then, they had to use chamber pots. The nearest supply of water was about a mile away.

To manage the White House servants, the Adamses relied on their steward, John Briesler. The next president, Thomas Jefferson, began the practice of having slaves do most of the household work in the White House. Even so, living in the Executive Mansion was very expensive. Jefferson liked to live well, and he enjoyed giving elegant dinner parties. He had to pay for them himself because the government did not yet pay for the president's personal staff or his official entertaining.

Thomas Jefferson

7

Dolley Madison

Like Thomas Jefferson, President James Madison and his wife, Dolley, loved to invite guests to lavish dinners and receptions. However, their parties were not held in the White House during the president's last years in office. The Madisons were forced to leave the White House during the War of 1812 (1812–1814) between the United States and Great Britain.

On August 24, 1814, First Lady Dolley Madison received a message that she should leave the Executive Mansion immediately

Dolley Madison's quick thinking saved this portrait of George Washington, by artist Gilbert Stuart, from destruction.

because British troops were advancing toward Washington. She quickly ordered her servants to collect valuables for her to take with her. They saved a famous Gilbert Stuart portrait of George Washington by removing the canvas from its frame. She also managed to rescue some government records and important documents, such as the Declaration of Independence.

Four hours later, British troops took over the White House. The officers drank President Madison's wine and collected souvenirs. Then their men set fire to the building, destroying the interior. Most of the outer walls were left standing. Three days later, the British left the area, and the Madisons returned to Washington. They rented a brick house, called the Octagon, while the Executive Mansion was reconstructed.

From 1815 to 1817, James Hoban supervised the rebuilding of the White House. He was able to hire many of the same people who had worked on it before. Most of the fire-blackened structure had to be demolished. Only the basement level was in good condition. Some of the outer walls were demolished and reconstructed. The new walls were made of sandstone from the Aquia quarry, in Virginia, just like the original walls. Once again, they were whitewashed.

The British set the White House ablaze during their attack on Washington, D.C.

It took ten years to build the first White House but only three to rebuild it. Hoban no longer had to wait while individual craftsmen created what was needed. Now he could purchase ready-made and less costly fireplace mantels and flooring. He also saved time by using newly invented steamboats instead of relying on horse-drawn carts to transport supplies.

When the renovations were completed in 1817, President James Monroe and his wife, Elizabeth, ordered expensive new furniture from France to replace what the British had burned. Congress complained bitterly. The lawmakers wanted the Monroes to purchase cheaper, plainer, American-made furnishings. To compromise, Monroe bought both French and American furniture.

A chair that President Monroe bought from an American furniture maker

Later presidents also had a difficult time convincing Congress to pay for redecorating the

White House. The lawmakers usually argued that refurbishing it was too costly. However, the state rooms were used constantly because all the official receptions were held there. When the furnishings wore out, replacements were necessary. After he took office in 1829, President Andrew Jackson succeeded in getting Congress to pay for remodeling the White House. He had the North Portico built in 1830 (the South Portico had been completed in 1824). In 1833, a system of pipes was installed to run water into the White House. A ground-floor bathing room with a shower was also added. At that time, indoor plumbing was considered a luxury. People do not know exactly when bathtubs and toilets were installed in the White House.

Throughout the 1800s, the White House was gradually modernized and made more comfortable. Presidential couples had only candles and oil lamps for light until 1848, when President James K. Polk had safer, cheaper gaslight installed. At a reception a few days later, First Lady Sarah Polk insisted on keeping candles in one chandelier. She said that she preferred the "wax candles shedding their soft radiance." At nine o'clock that evening, the gas company closed for the night, and the White House suddenly went dark—except for Sarah's chandelier.

Soon after the new lighting was installed, other improvements followed. In the 1850s, Millard and Abigail Fillmore introduced central heating to the cold and drafty mansion. They also ordered the first stove in the White House. Until then, all the cooking was done over open hearths with hooks holding pots and pans over the fire. By 1853, the second-floor bathtubs had hot and cold running water. First Lady Abigail Fillmore also started the White House Library.

Under Presidents Franklin Pierce and James Buchanan, a conservatory was added. This heated greenhouse was a quiet place for relaxation, and it also provided beautiful cut flowers and potted plants for the mansion. First

The White House library, where books by American authors and presidential papers are kept

Families enjoyed it until it was demolished in the early 1900s (when the West Wing was built).

Greenhouses on the east side of the White House in about 1900

During and after the American Civil War (1861–1865), presidential families continued to make changes to the White House. The Lincolns refused to have slaves working in the mansion. Instead, they hired servants. In 1866, President Andrew Johnson had a telegraph installed in his office. Three years later, First Lady Julia Grant had closets built. Until then, First Families had to hang their clothes on pegs or store them in chests and wardrobes. President Rutherford B. Hayes ordered telephones for the White House in 1877, after he and his wife Lucy watched a demonstration by inventor Alexander Graham Bell. Nicknamed "Elegant Arthur," President Chester A. Arthur had beautiful panels of Tiffany glass installed in the Entrance Hall. In 1881, he rode in the Executive Mansion's first elevator.

President Benjamin Harrison had the White House wired for electricity in 1891. This improvement made it possible for the household staff to use many electrical appliances, such as irons and vacuum cleaners. Nevertheless, the Harrisons were afraid of electrical shocks and did not want to touch the light switches. They ordered their servants to turn the lights on and off when the presidential couple entered or left a room.

Although many modern conveniences, such as electricity, improved the president's house during the 1800s, the size of the mansion had not changed much. Several presidents had asked Congress to enlarge the Executive Mansion, but their requests were denied. When President Theodore Roosevelt and his family moved into the White House in 1901, it was just over one hundred years old and in need of more rooms and repairs. The second floor of the building had only eight rooms—not enough space for the six Roosevelt children and their assorted pets. Offices for the president and his staff were also located on the second floor, so the family lacked privacy, too. Government officials and strangers seeking favors shared the same hallways as the First Family. "[I]t's like living over a store," President Roosevelt complained.

In 1902, Congress approved a major renovation of the Executive Mansion. The Roosevelts hired New York architect Charles F. McKim to head the project. While he enlarged the White House, they moved back to their New York home. McKim's company began work in July 1902, and by December, the renovation was completed.

Architects William Mead (left), Charles McKim (center), and Stanford White (right)

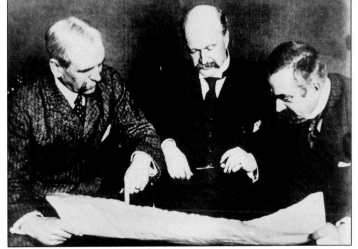

Within the White House, the State Dining
Room was expanded to seat more guests.
Theodore Roosevelt decorated it with the
heads of big-game animals he had hunted.
More important, McKim provided the First
Family with more bedrooms and living space
on the second floor. He moved the president's
staff offices to the nearby West Wing he had
just built.

The idea of adding wings to the White House
was not new, but earlier Congresses had
refused to pay for them. Although members
of the president's staff were relocated to the
West Wing, Roosevelt kept his own office
on the second floor of the White House.
Presidents had worked there since 1800.

First Lady Edith Roosevelt changed the management of the White House staff. She needed more time to watch her children. The young Roosevelts were often a handful. For example, they roller-skated in the East Room and slid down stairways on trays. One time, when Archibald Roosevelt was sick, his brother Quentin smuggled a pony into the White House elevator and up to Archibald's room for a visit. In 1903, Edith appointed the first Chief Usher, Thomas E. Stone, to supervise the household staff. Originally, ushers simply took visitors in to see the president and the First Lady, but soon they were running errands for the First Family as well. Today, the Chief Usher is the general manager of the White House with numerous important duties.

Archibald Roosevelt on his pony, Algonquin

Four men sit in the extra-large bathtub that was ordered for President Taft.

In 1909, the next president, William Howard Taft, had McKim double the size of the West Wing and build him an Oval Office at its center. Taft also added a garage for the new White House cars that replaced horses and carriages. Because he weighed more than 350 pounds (158 kilograms), an extra-large bathtub had to be brought to the White House for his use.

First Lady Helen Taft hired the first woman housekeeper at the White House, Elizabeth Jaffray. She worked at the White House from 1909 to 1926 (long after the Tafts had left), supervising the menus, marketing, cleaning, and laundry. Under the direction of the Chief Usher, she managed twenty-seven servants. (Today, the White House staff numbers about ninety people.)

Eager to save money, Nellie Taft ordered Elizabeth Jaffray to buy foods wholesale, or in large quantities. The Tafts even kept a cow, named Pauline Wayne, to keep them supplied with milk, butter, and cream. How relieved the First Family must have been in 1909, when

Congress agreed to pay the White House household staff. During Warren Harding's presidency (1921–1923), the government also began paying for official entertaining.

In addition, Congress approved money for improvements to the White House in the 1920s. In 1927, President Calvin Coolidge and his wife, Grace, had the roof and attic replaced to add a third story to the building. The extra space provided bedrooms for the staff and guests as well as more closets. The new third floor also included First Lady Grace Coolidge's "sky parlor," a comfortable room with magnificent views. Later presidential families renamed it the Solarium, or sun room.

Along with the expansion of the White House came another restoration. On Christmas Eve, 1929, President Herbert Hoover watched as a devastating fire destroyed the West Wing. He ordered his aides to save important papers, and he had them rescue a puppy that a secretary had hidden in an office as a surprise gift for his family. After the fire, Hoover had the West Wing rebuilt. He was also responsible for introducing radios to the mansion.

On December 24, 1929, firefighters work to put out a fire in the West Wing.

President Franklin D. Roosevelt and his wife, Eleanor, moved into the White House in 1933. They lived there for twelve years and left their mark on the building and the staff. President Roosevelt added an indoor swimming pool to the White House in 1933. He used it for exercise because after suffering from polio, he was paralyzed from the waist down. One year later, Roosevelt had the Oval Office moved to the

The Oval Office, where the president of the United States works

southeast corner of the West Wing, where it remains today. When the United States entered World War II in 1941, security was tightened. Guardhouses were erected at the outside gates, and visitors had to show passes to enter the grounds. President Roosevelt is credited with the construction of the modern East Wing in 1941, providing a bomb shelter, a movie theater, and more office space. By then, the West Wing had become overcrowded with presidential staff.

Guards at the gates of the White House (left) in the early 1940s

First Lady Eleanor Roosevelt also made changes in the Executive Mansion. She was amazed to discover how old-fashioned and unsanitary the kitchen was. In 1935, she modernized it with electric appliances, including the first dishwasher in the White House.

Henrietta Nesbitt

Eleanor Roosevelt was so busy with her activities as First Lady that she rarely had time for, or interest in, the household staff. As a result, housekeeper Henrietta Nesbitt ran the household to suit herself. Although the president liked fine food, the housekeeper insisted on having the cook prepare simple, bland meals—with one menu for each day of the week, repeated every week. When she was told that Franklin Delano Roosevelt hated broccoli, she ordered the cooks, "Fix it anyhow. He should like it."

After Roosevelt died in 1945, Harry Truman became president. Although the person who is president changes from time to time, the White House staff often remains the same from president to president. Sometimes this situation has caused problems. Henrietta Nesbitt still worked at the White House when the Trumans moved in, but she and the new First Lady, Bess Truman, disagreed about how the Executive Mansion should be run. There was a showdown between them when the housekeeper refused to give the First Lady a stick of butter to take to her club's pot-luck lunch—a meal where everyone brought something to share. Bess Truman had the Chief Usher fire Henrietta Nesbitt.

The Trumans changed more than the White House staff. President Truman was criticized for modifying the traditional appearance of the White House in 1948, when he added a balcony to the South Portico, outside his study. More important, he was responsible for another major reconstruction of the White House. Truman realized that the building was falling apart. In early 1948, the president wrote to his sister, "I've had the second floor where we live examined—and it is about to fall down! The engineer said that the ceiling in the State Dining Room only stayed up from force of habit!" Truman ordered the area shored up with pipes while experts examined the entire house. Then a piano in his daughter's sitting room broke through the floor. Congress voted to rebuild the White House, and the Trumans moved to nearby Blair House.

Harry and Bess Truman

During the Truman renovation, bulldozers dug a two-story basement in the White House.

On December 7, 1949, construction crews began their work. Only the third floor was structurally sound. Everything below it was removed piece by piece and numbered so that it could later be restored to its proper place. All that remained of the original building were the outside stone walls scarred by the fire in 1814. The work crews dug two new basement levels, providing a steel and concrete foundation for the building. When the job was completed, the White House grew from 62 to 100 rooms, from 26 hallways to 40, from 14 bathrooms to 19. The new basement levels had a barbershop, pantries, a laundry, and a staff kitchen. The mechanical and electrical systems were the best that 1950s technology could offer, including central air conditioning and fire alarms. The Trumans moved back to the White House on March 27, 1952.

Later presidential families found new purposes for some of the White House rooms. For example, in the 1960s, Grace Coolidge's "sky parlor" became the perfect setting for a kindergarten for Caroline Kennedy, the daughter of President John F. Kennedy and his wife, Jacqueline. Later, Lynda and Lucie Johnson, the daughters of Lyndon and "Lady Bird" Johnson, used it to "hang out" with their teenage friends.

Like so many presidents before him, Richard Nixon made changes to the White House too. He enjoyed bowling, so he had workers build a single-lane bowling alley. In 1969, Nixon had Franklin Roosevelt's swimming pool covered over and made into a pressroom for news reporters. In 1970, as a special surprise for her husband, First Lady Patricia Nixon had lights installed to illuminate the White House at night. She also suggested that ramps be built to make it easier for people in wheelchairs to visit the White House.

For the rest of the century, First Families continued to restore and modernize the White House. Gerald Ford had an outdoor pool built. Jimmy and Rosalynn Carter ordered some forty coats of paint removed from the outside walls. Then, the sandstone walls were repaired. In 1977, they ordered computers for the Executive Mansion. For their daughter, Amy, they had a treehouse built in a cedar tree on the South Lawn. In the 1980s, Ronald and Nancy Reagan added a visitors' entrance. George and Barbara Bush encouraged the use of energy-saving lights. In 1993, Bill and Hillary Clinton brought the White House into the information age with its own website.

On September 12, 1994, a firefighter hoses down the wreckage of a single-engine plane.

During Clinton's presidency, the pilot of a single-engine plane deliberately crashed into the South Lawn of the White House, and gunmen shot at the building. To better protect the people who lived and worked in the president's house, government officials closed off two blocks in front of the Executive Mansion to all traffic. Since May 20, 1995, people have entered the area only on foot.

No doubt, future presidents will continue to protect and preserve the White House. In 1998, the National Park Service outlined a twenty-year plan to renovate the White House once more. If Congress approves money for the plan, underground space would be added for parking, offices, and recreation. Outwardly, the building would be unchanged. Future presidents will probably have their own ideas about what should be done to improve their residence.

Despite all the remodeling and reconstruction, the White House has remained a fond and familiar sight to generations of Americans. For more than two hundred years, this beloved landmark has been the official home and office of their president. In 1800, after his first night in the Executive Mansion, John Adams wrote: "I Pray Heaven To Bestow THE BEST OF BLESSINGS ON This House And All that shall hereafter Inhabit it. May none but Honest and Wise Men ever rule under This Roof." His words are now found carved into the mantel in the State Dining Room. Hopefully, Adams's words will continue to inspire future presidents for another two hundred years.

John Adams wrote this blessing in hopes of encouraging good fortune for the White House and future presidents.

FUN FACTS ABOUT

- The first child to live in the White House was Susanna, the four-year-old granddaughter of John and Abigail Adams.

- The First Family lives on the second floor of the White House. The Lincoln Bedroom is also on the second floor. Guests of the First Family often stay overnight in the Lincoln Bedroom. President Abraham Lincoln used this room as an office.

- Officially, the president's home was known as the Executive Mansion because the president was the nation's chief executive. Most people, however, referred to the mansion as the "President's House." In 1798, the outer walls were whitewashed, and the public began calling it the "White House." In November 1810, the nickname the "White House," was written for the first time in a Baltimore, Maryland, newspaper. The name stuck. In 1901, President Theodore Roosevelt made it the building's official title.

- Holiday events at the White House include the annual Easter Egg Roll—always held on the Monday after Easter—and the lighting of the national Christmas tree.

- The White House is open to the public, but in the past, security was sometimes a problem. In the 1890s, First Lady Frances Cleveland ordered policemen to keep tourists from strolling on White House lawns. One of them had picked up her baby daughter Ruth and passed her around despite pleas from Ruth's nurse. Another time, a sightseer tried to cut off one of the child's hair curls as a souvenir.

THE WHITE HOUSE

- First Ladies sometimes made difficult demands of the staff. First Lady Lou Henry Hoover insisted that the servants disappear from sight whenever she and the president entered a room. First Lady Bess Truman did not like dust, and she reminded the maids to wipe the woodwork every day. First Lady Mamie Eisenhower made the staff vacuum the White House carpets over and over again because she did not want any footprints on the rugs.

- The White House was the largest house in the United States until the 1870s.

- To take a tour of the White House, visitors need to get free tickets. Some lucky people who get them wait in line for hours. Others get tickets from members of Congress. On the tour, visitors see rooms on the Ground Floor and the State Floor.

- Visit the White House website at this address:
  http://www.whitehouse.gov
  The "White House for Kids" link includes information on the location and history of the White House, the president, children in the White House, and White House pets.

- The White House received its first e-mail message on June 1, 1993. In February 1999, the president received over 50,000 e-mails in one five-day period. Usually, he receives from 2,000 to 5,000 electronic messages per day. Anyone can e-mail the president and vice president of the United States at the following addresses:

  president@whitehouse.gov
  vice.president@whitehouse.gov

GLOSSARY

William Mead, Charles McKim and Stanford White were architects for the White House renovation in 1902.

architect – a person who designs buildings and oversees their construction

capital – a city where a state or national government is located

chamber pot – a pan kept in bedrooms for toilet needs

Chief Usher – the general manager of the White House, this person escorts important visitors, supervises the staff, maintains the house and grounds, and prepares the budget for the Executive Mansion

Congress – the United States Senate and House of Representatives

First Lady – wife of the president of the United States or his official hostess if he is a bachelor or a widower

plantation – a large farm in the southern United States

portico – a porch or walkway with a roof that is supported by a row of columns

reception – a social gathering honoring or introducing someone

renovation – the renewal or restoration of a building or room

staff – a group of assistants

steward – a person who manages another person's household or property

wing – a part of a building that sticks out from the main structure

The South Portico

TIMELINE

James Hoban
wins design
competition

Renovations
completed;
Monroes order
new furniture

1792

1800 *November 1:* John and
Abigail Adams move in

1814 White House destroyed by fire

1817

1824 South Portico completed

1830 North Portico completed

1848 Gaslight replaces candles

Telephones installed **1877**

1891 Electricity installed

West Wing added **1902**

1903

Thomas E. Stone
becomes first Chief Usher

Elizabeth Jaffray becomes first **1909**
White House housekeeper

Third floor and "sky parlor" built **1927**

1929

White House kitchen modernized **1935**

Truman Balcony erected **1948**

1949

1952

December 24:
Fire destroys
West Wing

1970 White House illuminated at night

1977

White House
gutted and
reconstructed

Exterior paint
removed;
sandstone walls
repaired; first
White House
computers
ordered

1993 White House website goes online

2000 Bicentennial anniversary

INDEX *(Boldface page numbers indicate illustrations.)*

PHOTO CREDITS

Photographs ©: AP/Wide World Photos: 26 (Doug Mills), 22; Archive Photos: 15, 30 top; Corbis-Bettmann: 7, 19, 21, 31 center; Culver Pictures: 18; Library of Congress: 13, 14 (Jay Malin), 16 left; National Park Service, cover; North Wind Picture Archives: 4, 9; Stock Montage, Inc.: 17; Tom Dietrich: 1, 28, 29, 30 bottom; White House Historical Association: 8 bottom (National Geographic Society), 2, 5, 6, 8 top, 10, 12, 16 right, 20, 23, 27, 31 top.

PICTURE IDENTIFICATIONS

Cover: After layers of old exterior paint were removed and the sandstone was restored, painters apply a coat of white paint to the White House in May 1981. It takes 570 gallons of white paint to cover the exterior of the White House. Page 1: The South Portico of the White House. Page 2: The Blue Room, where the president often hosts receptions.

ABOUT THE AUTHOR

Barbara Silberdick Feinberg graduated with honors from Wellesley College, where she was elected to Phi Beta Kappa. She holds a Ph.D. in political science from Yale University. She has written other books for Children's Press, including *Bess Wallace Truman*, *Edith Kermit Carow Roosevelt*, *Patricia Ryan Nixon*, and *Hiroshima and Nagasaki*. She lives in New York City with her Yorkshire terrier, Holly. Among her hobbies are growing African violets, collecting autographs of historical personalities, listening to the popular music of the 1920s, 1930s, and 1940s, and working out in exercise classes.